Gentlemen of the Ri

the Last Coracle men of the Severn G

Phyllis Blakemore

This book is dedicated to the memory of Tommy Rogers, his sons. Jimmy and Harry Rogers, and his grandson Eustace Rogers, always known as Eusty. These men braved the River Severn in times of devastating flood. They set out in their coracles to assist or rescue families cut off by the rising water. They used no life jackets, and there were no helicopters overhead to help. The Rogers family have a history of coracle making, which goes back over 250 years, long before the famous Ironbridge was built. A tradition of which they can be justly proud.

Other coraclemen lived in Ironbridge up to the middle of the 20th century, and they too saved lives and did a great service to the community. The wives, mothers and sisters of the coracle men spent many anxious hours awaiting the return of their menfolk. The coracle men could not have carried out the work they did, without the support of their families.

SOURCES

Many of the tales of Tommy Rogers and his sons Jimmy and Harry, are taken from the Ironbridge Histories written some years ago by the late Leonard Beeston, and loaned to me by his sister, Mrs. G. Edwards.

I have less material about Jimmy Rogers, as he went to live in Canada for some years.

Some of Leonard's stories are identical to those which have appeared in various publications since the 1930s, but there is no possibility whatsoever of plagiarism. The coracle men were very sociable people, and loved to talk to visitors about their lives by the river and their coracles. The stories were told many times over to different people. Leonard Beeston was a great friend of Eusty Rogers, and he heard these stories at first hand.

For my part I spent many hours in Ironbridge with Eusty, in his home and in his workshop. I used no tape recorder or made notes. The time spent with him was so fascinating I just wanted to look and listen. I hope that I have related as near as possible all he told me on those summer evenings in Ironbridge.

Harry and Jimmy Rogers with a miniature coracle made for Canadian relations.

ACKNOWLEDGEMENTS

I would like to thank my daughter Mrs. Diane Perry for valuable assistance in editing, advice and constant encouragement. Grateful thanks also to Mrs. Alice Arrowsmith, daughter of the late Harry Rogers, and to Mrs. Margaret Seaton-Smith and Mrs. Kathleen Watkiss, his granddaughters, for their help and approval. Thanks are also due to Mrs. Gertrude Edwards, for the loan of the Ironbridge Histories written by her brother, the late Leonard Beeston.

Many thanks to Mr. Paul France, for the wonderful photographs, and to Mr. Toby Neal of the Shropshire Star for his advice and encouragement. Also to Doreen of the Photographic Department of the Shropshire Star for her contribution regarding the pictures. Thanks to Mr. Simon Whaley for his advice, and to Mrs. Selina Ormond for the excellent typing out of my manuscript. Also to Jean Henderson, Dab Hands, for additional typing, and to Mrs. Vera Chetwood: for her support.

I would also like to express my thanks and appreciation to Mrs. Judy Walker and staff at the Green Wood Centre, Coalbrookdale for their assistance and information supplied.

INTRODUCTION

At one time the coracle was a familiar sight on the river at Ironbridge in Shropshire. Up to the late 1980s visitors on a summer's day would see the craft paddled effortlessly on tranquil water, and some of them toyed with the idea of owning one of these interesting little boats.

The Ironbridge Coracle Man usually had one for sale, but the first question he asked a prospective buyer was "Con yer swim?" The skilfully constructed, but somewhat fragile looking boat was not easy to handle unless "you were brought up with it" he would tell them.

For centuries the coracle has been in use on British rivers. When Julius Caesar arrived here in 55 B.C. he noticed 'wicker boats', manned by the inhabitants, the Ancient Britons. The coracle has a long and interesting history. From Roman times, through the Saxon period, to Medieval monks, and on into later centuries, this small boat has been invaluable to the rural and riverside people of Britain and Ireland. Up to the 1950s the coracle was still being used as a working boat in many country areas. In Wales it is seen on the rivers, including the Teifi and the Dee, and in Shropshire on the Severn. The Welsh coracle is a different shape from the Shropshire type. It has a broader 'back' whereas the Shropshire coracle is more oval and has been described many times as being like 'one half of a walnut shell'. Coracle racing has been revived in some rural parts of the country, but it is now more for entertainment at regattas or Bank Holiday entertainment.

In the 1770s the coracle men who lived by the riverside in the Severn Gorge had a ringside view of a remarkable event which was to take place. The area was then called Madeley Wood, near Coalbrookdale. A bridge was urgently needed over the river and it was to be a special bridge, the first in the world to be cast in iron. The bridge was erected in 1779, and the man who masterminded this wonderful feat of engineering was Abraham Darby. The bridge combined strength with beauty, and the world came to gaze and wonder and admire. Artists came to paint pictures of the bridge and in their pictures they showed trows and barges sailing under its massive arches. The artists often included in their pictures a smaller craft, the coracle, bobbing bravely around the larger heavier vessels.

On this stretch of river which flows through Ironbridge, there was a Dynasty of Coracle Makers. The Rogers family had constructed and used these boats for generations certainly for over 250 years. They and other riverside dwellers would have seen the progress of the bridge from its earliest stage, seen the scaffolding go up, and watched as the iron ribs were hauled into place using horse power and a skilful workforce. In 1779 they witnessed its completion.

Life would change forever for the families in the vicinity of the bridge as it was to become a wonder of the world. The benefit of having a bridge in this particular place was immense; no longer did goods have to be carted miles up or down the river to the nearest bridge. Madeley Wood now had its own magnificent bridge, and the town was later to be known as Ironbridge.

The Rogers family and other coracle men knew the river better than anyone. They fished from it, they saved lives from drowning, and they ferried people across it, as the toll was often too high for the poorer people. When a decline in industry and unemployment came to the valley, these men formed a band of poachers in order to provide food for the large and hungry families. They were all highly respected members of the community. They were the 'Gentlemen of the River'.

Eusty Rogers

On a summer's evening in the late 1980s I went down to Ironbridge to meet the last Coracle Man of the Severn Gorge. When I arrived in Ironbridge that evening the sun was about to set; it was a brilliant ball of crimson and its radiance almost unearthly. It seemed as if the entire valley was lit up by a vast furnace, not difficult to imagine here, where in centuries past, furnaces glowed fiercely and illuminated the sky, here where the Industrial Revolution thundered its way into a sleepy valley. I was going to meet Eusty Rogers, a man who knew the Severn in all its moods. Its fearsome floods or its dangerous undercurrents held no fear for him.

I left the Bridge and walked up the deserted High Street; the visitors had gone, the shops and cafes were closed. I went down the Dip as it is known locally, a narrow passageway between tall buildings, which led to Severnside and there leaning on the railings was Eusty with two of his friends. All day, people from all over the world had thronged into the small market town of

Eusty with Phyllis Blakemore, 1984 (photo Paul Bond).

Eusty's Workshop.

Ironbridge. They had come to see the majestic bridge, as people had done for over 200 years. We chatted for a while then Eusty invited me to see his workshop, built precariously on the river bank.

It was a fascinating jumble of tools some of which were in every day use, together with relics of the past. The walls, floor and bench were crowded with artefacts. Eusty pointed out old paddles, (called spades by the coracle men) and showed me ancient walking sticks carved with bird and animal heads. One corner of the workshop was crammed with fishing rods, nets and waders. In another I saw scythes, rakes, axes, and chains. The floor was strewn with wicker baskets, rabbit nets, mole and rat traps. Over it all was a pleasant smell of tar, oil, rope and freshly sawn wood. Although it looked like a jumble, Eusty knew where everything was, and patiently answered my many questions, except for the ring of rope! This was a circle about eight inches in diameter, made from tightly woven rope. I turned it over and over many times, trying to find the join.

"How was it made?" I asked.

Laughing, he said "I am not going to tell you!" Nor would he.

Nearby were some long white poles. I asked Eusty what they were used for. He said they were for locating the bodies of people drowned in the river and explained how this was done. Eusty would get a rowing boat in midstream. On each side of the river would be a policeman steadying the boat with ropes. As the boat went slowly with the flow of water Eusty would feel down as far as possible with the pole. He told me: "You always knew when the pole touched a dead body. You knew it was that and could be nothing else." A great many bodies have been recovered by the Rogers family over the years. It is a family tradition that they do not ask for payment for this grim task, and it is a tradition that has never wavered.

Eusty, 1984 (photo Paul Bond).

Eusty Rogers, c.1986 (photo Phyllis Blakemore)

We left the workshop and went into Eusty's cottage, as he had promised to show me the family Bible. Various entries had been made. On the first page I read:

THOMAS ROGERS	Born 1778	Died 1827
BEN ROGERS	Born 1804	Died 1848
TOMMY ROGERS	Born 1843	Died 1924

Tommy's elder son Jimmy was born in 1886, his younger son Harry in 1887 and Harry's son Eustace (always called Eusty) was born in 1914 just before World War One.

Eusty pointed out two brass candlesticks. Each one was mounted on a horse's foot. The hooves had been preserved and polished. On the base was a brass horseshoe, complete with nails. Apparently after the death of a favourite hunter owned by the local squire the hooves had been removed and made into candlesticks and presented to a member of the Rogers family.

Tommy Rogers - 1843-1924

I wanted to know more about the old days, so Eusty began with his grandfather, the unique Tommy Rogers. When Tommy Rogers was born in 1843 the famous bridge was just 64 years old. People were still coming to see it and admire its elegant structure. Tommy was one of the several sons of Ben and Mary Rogers of Severnside and he was to become one of Ironbridge's most colourful and respected characters.

The family home was just a few yards from the Iron Bridge and history was all around. On the opposite side of the river was the Great Wheel of Benthall. Built around 1799, it was 50 feet in diameter. Also from their cottage the Rogers children could see the Benthall Boatyard where the famous trow 'William' was built in 1801 and which was sunk in the Bristol Channel in 1939.

By the time Tommy was 21 he knew more about the river and the surrounding countryside than anyone. He grew up to be a strong fearless man, able to tackle anything. It was said he weighed nearly 20 stone. He carried on the family tradition of coracle making and was not only an expert in the handling of this craft; he also navigated the river on barges, trows, punts and rowing boats. His rivercraft was learned from his family and from the old watermen who thronged the Ironbridge area in those days.

He married and he, with his wife Susannah and their children, lived in the family cottage on Severnside, home to many generations of Rogers coracle men. They had two sons, Jimmy and Harry, and two daughters, Janet and May who later emigrated to Canada. During his lifetime. Tommy saved eight people from drowning and had recovered 30 bodies from the treacherous waters of the Severn Gorge. To these unfortunate victims the river must have looked very inviting on a hot summer's day. They did not realise that there were dangerous undercurrents, and they would soon get into difficulties. The Rogers men knew every yard of the river, where it was shallow or deep and where the undercurrents were. Their knowledge of the river was phenomenal.

**Steam tug *Christiana* by the Bower Yard ironbridge, *c.*1860
Courtesy of the Ironbridge Museum Trust.**

Tommy's skill in rivercraft and his acts of bravery were greatly appreciated and the local authorities presented him with a silver watch. He was very proud of this watch and wore it on a chain across his chest. Tommy was fond of a few pints of beer and one night he was in the Golden Ball on Madeley Wood, drinking with his friends. As the evening wore on, and more beer was consumed, he began to show off about his watch. In those far off days the area round The Golden Ball was known locally as 'Thief Street' and before the night was out Tommy had been relieved of his greatly prized watch. When he sobered up he made extensive inquiries but the watch was never seen again. It was fortunate for the thief that Tommy Rogers did not find him. He was greatly saddened by the loss and wished he had been more careful.

Some months later a wealthy old gentleman was on holiday in Ironbridge. He had heard about Tommy Rogers and his acts of bravery and also of the loss of his silver watch. The kind-hearted old man went to see Tommy and insisted that he should accept his own silver watch. The coracle man refused at first, as of course it was not the same as being presented with a watch for bravery, but the visitor was so impressed with Tommy that he insisted and at last he gratefully accepted the watch. He wore it across his chest as before and vowed he would keep this one safe.

Once again bad luck was round the corner. One blustery day he was out in his coracle and a freak storm blew up. Now Tommy could deal with the roughest of weather but the wave which hit him was immense and the coracle capsized. The overturning did not bother Tommy as he was a strong swimmer, and in minutes he had got the boat the right way up again, but he glanced down at his waistcoat and to his horror the watch was missing. The force of the wave had caused it to become detached and it now lay at the bottom of the Severn. He could hardly believe his bad luck, but knowing the river was not particularly deep where he had overturned, he was determined to try and recover the watch.

The next day the storm had subsided and with his two sons. Jimmy and Harry, he set about diving for the watch. It took Tommy and his boys three days of plunging down to the river bed to search for the watch. Imagine their relief when they found it half-submerged in the mud at the bottom of the river. Recovering the watch had taken determination, courage and physical stamina. Tommy and his sons possessed all of these.

7

In Victorian times Ironbridge had an annual fair. This was held in front of the old Bedlam Furnaces along Waterloo Street. In addition to swing boats and coconut shies there was usually a boxing booth. Local youths were invited to step into the ring and take on one of the travelling boxers. If they won they would get the prize money. Most of the local boys did not stand a chance against these beefy fairground men, bouncing round the ring punching the air showing off their skills. Then Tommy Rogers would heave his immensely fit twenty stone over the ropes. The onlookers would watch with glee, because they knew what was going to happen! Many a professional boxer left Ironbridge having had a good hiding from Tommy.

**Severn Warehouse, Ironbridge.
Courtesy of the Ironbridge Museum Trust.**

In 1875 Captain Mathew Webb was successful in swimming the English Channel. Mathew's family had lived at Dawley, Shropshire, but later moved to Ironbridge. The schoolboy Mathew used to practise swimming in the Severn with Tommy Rogers, who gave him hints. Mathew would swim for long periods against a strong current, which would stand him in good stead for when he attempted the Channel in years to come.

After his successful Channel crossing. Captain Webb returned to Shropshire. He was met at Wellington and when he arrived at Coalbrookdale, a triumphal arch had been erected, bands played, torches carried and the crowds turned out to welcome their hero. Tommy Rogers proudly watched the spectacle, knowing he had been part of the Captain's training.

**Severn Trow near to the Coalport china works, *c.*1890.
Courtesy of the Ironbridge Museum Trust.**

In 1895 Tommy took the last barge from Ironbridge bound for Gloucester. River traffic had declined since the coming of the railway line in the 1840s so this was to have been a momentous journey, which it was but not in the way that had been planned. The barge was loaded with 80 tons of bricks from the Ladywood Brickworks, which was opposite Tommy's house. His son Harry, then just eight years, old was to accompany him as cabin boy on this last journey for the old barge. Tommy was an expert bargeman and had taken numerous barges down the Severn, but just as the vessel reached Bridgnorth, a storm, which had followed them down river, broke directly over them. The river became turbulent with rough waves and high wind. In spite of skilful manoeuvring, the barge collided with the abutments of the bridge.

The barge sank, taking with it the 80 tons of bricks where they lie to this day. Tommy and his son were able to swim to the riverbank to safety, but were disappointed, as the opportunity to sail downstream with one of the old barges had gone forever.

Shortly after this disaster Tommy was asked to take a barge upstream to Shrewsbury. A retired colonel required it to be moored near his home. It was the last barge to be taken up river. This time it had to be towed, so Tommy hired a horse. He took his son Harry again and a friend called Gambler Baugh. It was not going to be an easy task. Since the coming of the railway the towpaths had become overgrown as very few people now used them.

Tommy, Harry and Gambler Baugh hacked and trampled their way up the side of the river making way for the horse to pull the barge. At Leighton, a few miles upstream, he was met by the landowner, a policeman and a gamekeeper. Tommy was told he could not continue as the path ran through the landowner's property. He insisted that he had a job to do, and was going to do it. Angry voices were raised and strong language used. The argument became very heated. Tommy made a decision and without more ado he hitched the horse to 40 yards of fencing and pulled it clean out of the ground. He then calmly put the horse back on the barge chain and continued on his way, shouting over his shoulder and laughing "The Colonel said 'remove all obstacles!'" The barge was delivered to the mooring at Shrewsbury and nothing more was heard of the incident. It is more than likely that the landowner and the Colonel knew each other socially and when they met would probably laugh as heartily as Tommy Rogers.

The viaduct opposite the Severn Warehouse Coalbrookdale. It was the route of the Great Western Railway line to Shrewsbury from the Severn Valley. In World War II, a German bomber dropped three bombs in the woods above failing in an attempt to sever the rail line.

In the 1840s and 1850s the Great Western Railway extended its lines over a wide area, so the river traffic declined dramatically. Industry in the area also declined. The zenith of trade had been in the two hundred years before Tommy Rogers was born. There was large scale unemployment and where there was work to be had, wages were low. The working class people here of Ironbridge in those days had very large families, sometimes up to ten or more children. The men stood by the Penniless Rails by the Market Square while the mothers at home were hard-pressed to find food and clothes for the family. The cottages they lived in were in a poor state of repair, with cramped conditions, often damp and several families had to share an earth lavatory. In 1840 cholera broke out in the district and in one part of Ironbridge, 32 people died.

With bad housing conditions, disease and unemployment it was a depressing time for the poorer families of the area, but there was always a great community spirit and they helped each other whenever possible. Eventually the situation became desperate and in order to provide food for the large families a band of poachers was formed.

Their names conjure up some very colourful characters: Fussler Potts, Bunkus Owen, Hell Fire Jack, Timmy Lynall, Dick the Keen-Un, Gambler Baugh, Big Neddy, Little Neddy, Gunner Boden, Bill Humphries, Johnny Thompson, Trevis, Pottery George, Nacky Brady, and John (The Major) Goodwin. The leader of this band of men was Tommy Rogers. There were Broseley and Much Wenlock poachers also, as there was poverty on either side of the river. The Chippy Haileys were the Broseley poachers. They were all experienced coracle men, countrymen, fearless and dedicated and braved the river in all its moods; they faced gamekeepers with guns, and were hounded by the police, whom they called 'Peelers' or 'Bluebottles'.

Some of the men were caught and served prison sentences. This must have been purgatory for them, to be locked in a cell looking at daylight through bars and the only exercise a walk in the prison yard. Their way of life was in the woods, the fields and on the river. They knew the dangers, but were willing to risk their freedom in order to put meals on the tables for the hungry families. They were aware that they were robbing the rich to feed the poor, but their logic was that the fields were full of rabbits, in the woods there was an abundance of pheasants and the Severn was teeming with fish. They quite simply hunted for food regardless of the consequences.

The poachers went out in groups of two or three in the dead of night. If they met someone they did not speak, nor answer if spoken to so as not to implicate anyone else. If the poaching was up river they carried their coracle over their backs with the strap pulled across their chest. In his 'History of Madeley' John Randall, the Victorian historian said 'They must have looked like enormous beetles.' When they had done their night's work they would load the nets and catch of rabbits into the coracle and glide silently down the dark river.

They were dedicated to the job and completely fearless, but they all had different personalities. Bill Humphries never got caught. He looked nothing like a poacher. During the day he always wore a smart suit with watch and chain, a bowler hat and carried a walking cane. He would stroll for miles around the country lanes and park land, making a mental note of the places he considered would be plentiful in game and would convey this valuable information to the other poachers who found his 'spying' of great assistance.

Dick the Keen-Un was a very small man and an expert poacher, who rarely got caught. He could almost scent a gamekeeper or a 'Peeler' and being so small he could conceal himself in the most unlikely places and then creep out of his hiding place when the coast was clear. Dick had a bad fault however; he was too fond of his beer. He was a very heavy drinker and the other poachers were concerned that when Dick was 'in his cups' he would let out important information. He never did, but there was always the fear that he might.

One night in The White Hart on the Wharfage, Dick got very drunk. He became troublesome and made a nuisance of himself. The landlord had no choice but to throw him out. Dick wanted revenge and due to his very small build he was able to conceal himself on the premises. In the middle of the night when the landlord was asleep Dick crept through a small door, or hatch, which led to the cellar. There he turned on all the taps on the beer barrels. The beer flowed out on to the cellar floor and Dick disappeared into the night. When the landlord found his flooded cellar next morning he must have guessed who was responsible. No one else could have got through such a small space but nothing could be proved and Dick the Keen-Un got away with it.

Middle - Dick-the-Keen-Un
(poacher *c.*1910) others unknown.

Nacky Brady was another character. He was a tall man and excellent poacher. He too liked a drink and one day he had too much at a public house in Buildwas. He fell asleep in the undergrowth at the side of the river. Two schoolboys were up around Buildwas, looking for moorhen eggs. They saw Nacky lying in the bushes and ran down to Ironbridge to find Tommy Rogers.

"Nacky is dead" they told Tommy, "He's lying by the river."

"Dead drunk more like" said Tommy and went off to find Gambler Baugh. Tommy and Gambler went off up the river and located Nacky. Tommy got hold of his legs and Gambler took hold of his arms. With a "One, Two, Three!" they swung him into the shallow part of the river. Nacky came up spluttering and swearing, but in a short time sobered up and happily walked off home with his two good friends.

Tommy Rogers, near to Buildwas Abbey c.1920.

There was a great loyalty between the poachers. It was an unwritten law they would never give each other away to the police. A man would rather go to prison for something he was not guilty of, rather than 'grass' on a fellow poacher. When the poachers had had a good night's catch of rabbits, or perhaps pheasants and sometimes salmon, they had to be careful where they unloaded. A good drop off place was at Cressage, up river from Ironbridge. They would take the game to a friend who stored it in his 'brewhouse'. Next morning the friend packed it into a wicker hamper and took it to Cressage Station to be transported on the first train down to Ironbridge. People sent pigeons and other poultry in wicker baskets so it did not arouse any suspicion. When the hamper arrived at Ironbridge Station, a porter who was 'in the know' would wheel it across the bridge and deliver it to one of the poacher's homes for collection by the Ironbridge housewives. The women all wore long skirts in those days and could easily conceal a rabbit or pheasant under them. After collection the women would casually walk homewards, probably saying "Good morning" as they passed the local "bobby". With a few vegetables from their garden there would be a tasty meal on the table that night. The poachers themselves could conceal a couple of rabbits in their large 'poachers pockets'. They would have prearranged dropping off places such as the barbers or a pub backyard and the game was soon collected.

The wife of one of the poachers had a novel way of getting game to her friends and neighbours. She carried a wicker basket on top of which was an array of cotton, ribbon, elastic, safety pins and such like. Underneath would be a fine plump rabbit for the cooking pot. When the rabbit had been skinned and was being prepared for cooking the children of the house would take the rabbit skin to the local rag and bone man who gave them a halfpenny.

John Goodwin (The Major) was an expert coracle man and a strong swimmer, but he came to grief in a mysterious way. One dark night he came down the river in his coracle and pulled in by the Severn. A policeman was watching. As The Major was about to get out of the coracle, the policeman rushed into the shallow water and tipped the coracle up. What happened after that is not known as it was not reported, but The Major's body was found next day. There may have been a fight, but it was recorded as 'accidental death'.

Nacky Brady had a similar experience but he did not drown. He pulled his coracle in by the Lakeshead Tavern in Waterloo Street. A 'Peeler' jumped out and turned Nacky's coracle over. Nacky, strong and fit, immediately swam across the river, climbed on to the river bank and walked back up to Ironbridge. He knocked on Tommy Roger's door and asked if Tommy would please get his coracle back for him when it was light, as he himself was going into hiding. Next morning Tommy went down river and found Nacky's coracle. It was upside down, with an air pocket under it and still contained the night catch of game.

Fussler Potts was another one of the band of poachers. He was a big man, but had the ability to conceal himself from the police and gamekeepers. He would lie for hours until the coast was clear. He managed to get into what seemed to be inaccessible places. One day he gained entry into a shop and stole three choice hams. Undecided as to whom he should give the hams, he hid them under a bowl in a friend's garden. By now the police had been alerted. They suspected Fussler and arrested him. Meanwhile the friend had discovered the hams and heard of Fussler's arrest. Thinking quickly he put the hams in a sack, weighted it down and hung it from a bush into the river. The police went looking for the hams but could not find them.

At Fussler's trial it was thought he had got into the shop through a skylight. The solicitor defending him went to the shop and measured the skylight. In court next day he said it would have been impossible for a man of Fussler's size to get through the skylight. Fussler said nothing. He was found "Not Guilty", the hams were retrieved and shared.

One of the tales the river local people like to relate is of two friends who came toIronbridge for a day's fishing. They were not very experienced anglers and hired a punt and set off from Buildwas. Feeling hungry they called at a pub and feasted well, including quite a lot to drink. They got back in the punt and floated happily downstream. Not having much luck with the fishing, they drew near a man in a coracle, who showed the visitors the amount of fish he had caught. One of the visitors, eager to try his hand, plied the coracle man with money in exchange for a 'go' in his coracle. He knew nothing about the risks of fishing from a coracle, but was determined to try. With his fishing rod in one hand and the coracle paddle in the other, he floated off trying to steer the boat and fish at the same time.

Nacky Brady - poacher and basket maker c.1910.

In his tipsy state the fisherman got confused and accidentally dropped the paddle in the water, where it floated away. He kept hold of the fishing rod but then had no control over the coracle. At first it went straight down river, but then began to turn round and round as if attached to something under the water. Unknown to the fisherman there lurked in this part of the river, a monstrous pike. No one had ever been able to catch it, but it was believed to be very old and very large. It had taken hold of the angler's bait and got caught on the hook and was swimming round under the boat trying to free itself. Eventually it decided to swim downstream, still attached to the line. Because of its strength it pulled the coracle with it. The fisherman was terrified as he saw its huge head cutting the water in front of him. In his terror he dropped the rod and the pike freed itself.

By now the fisherman, white-faced, was being whirled down the Severn in a flimsy boat and with no paddle. Gently punting along behind him was the coracle man, who could hardly stand for laughing. The other fisherman with him began to get worried about his friend, so the riverman punted quickly alongside the victim and dragged the man and the coracle on to the punt and to safety. The fisherman had sobered up completely by then.

When Tommy Rogers was in his prime, winning boxing matches and coracle and punt races, he had a young supporter by the name of Charlie Roberts. To Charlie, Tommy Rogers was a hero, and at all the events Tommy entered, Charlie was there to cheer him on. When Charlie Roberts left school he went to work as a junior reporter on a local newspaper, possibly the 'Wellington Journal and Shrewsbury News' or the local newspaper 'The Ironbridge Chronicle'. He went to live in Accrington, and became a senior reporter on a Manchester newspaper. Even though living away from Ironbridge he never forgot his hero, Tommy Rogers, and when it was Tommy and Susannah's Golden Wedding, Charlie Roberts wrote the following verse to commemorate the event:

Good morning to you Tom, 'Old Boy',
By Jove - You're looking well,
Though people sometimes tell us,
That our looks the truth don't tell.

But when one's lived o'ver seventy years,
(That's Man's allotted span)
They seldom feel as once they did,
That's part of Nature's plan.

Yet, on and on, through months and years,
And partings by the way,
In health and strength you're spared to see,
Your Golden Wedding Day.

And so to you, your good wife too,
Your mate for fifty years,
The best of wishes I express,
And give three hearty cheers.

Your path has led through varied scenes,
I'm sure you will admit,
And if we asked, 'Have you seen life?'
You'd answer 'Just a bit'.

I here would reminiscent be,
Of times which were sublime,
When I was only quite a lad,
And you were in your prime.

How when the Annual Fete came round,
We watched the swimming race,
And to the joy of all the lads,
You often had first place.

In race with coracle or punt,
None with you could compare,
And after starting you from scratch,
You'd beat them fair and square.

I've often seen you use the gloves,
And your opponents trounce,
Some came with the 'Boxing Booths'
And had quite a lot of bounce.

At hunting game, you've also been,
A cracksman in your time,
And many a home has blessed your skill,
When they've sat down to dine.

Of nectar you've had your share,
And various brands you've tried,
And many Beanos you have had,
Down by the Severn-side.

And through the years that still remain,
To you and your dear spouse,
May fortune shine upon you,
And each member of your house.

And when from this world's scene you pass,
When this life's cares are o'er,
May all meet in the house at last,
Upon that happier Shore.

Although the poachers were taking game from the woods and fields of the local gentry, one squire of a nearby village had great respect for Tommy Rogers and his countryside skills. When the squire felt like some lively company he would instruct his coachman, Mr. Fletcher: "Go down to Ironbridge and bring Tommy Rogers back with you." The squire and poacher would then sit together in the village inn enjoying a drink and each other's company. The squire would no doubt learn quite a lot about his own woods and spinneys from Tommy. At the end of the evening, the coachman was instructed to take Tommy back home to Ironbridge in style in the squire's elegant family coach. The next night Tommy and friends would most likely be out netting rabbits in the squire's woods, but it was an arrangement which seemed to suit both countrymen. In fact it was this same squire whose railings Tommy tore up out of the ground when he was taking the barge up to Shrewsbury from Ironbridge. There were obviously no hard feelings.

In old age Tommy was still a strong swimmer and expert diver. One year he decided he would enter the diving competition which was to be held at the annual Ironbridge Regatta. He plunged into the water and disappeared without a ripple. The crowd waited... and waited... No sign of Tommy. People began to get worried. Someone ran down to Ironbridge to his home to break the dreadful news, but the family did not seem unduly worried, knowing Tommy's tricks of old. When the messenger arrived back at the Regatta field he found the crowd happy and relieved. Tommy Rogers was quite safe and enjoying the situation. He had dived in, and then swimming under water had surfaced further down river out of sight. He crept on to the river bank and hid under a withy bush, where he sat watching the panic he had caused. They forgave him his little joke. He was a popular man.

Also when in his late seventies, he had been standing outside his cottage when an unmanned boat came swirling down the Severn. In spite of his family's protests he launched his coracle and sped off in pursuit of the boat. He caught up with it, grabbed hold of it and paddled to the side of the river where he secured it to a tree. He slung his coracle over his back and sauntered back home none the worse for this escapade.

The Crooked S, Leighton Bank, between Buildwas and Cressace. In times of severe flooding this becomes one vast lake. (photo Paul Bond 1983)

The Rogers family home was an ancient cottage with beams, low ceilings and a narrow twisted staircase. Towards the end of his life Tommy had to take to his bed, which must have been devasting for such an active man. He knew the end was not far away. He called to his two sons. Jimmy and Harry. "Now my bonny lads," he said. "I am about to pass over to the other side. When you put me in my coffin you are going to have one hell of a job to get me down the stairs. So take me down now and put me in my chair by the fire." His sons gently carried their old father down and settled him in his chair.

"Right," said Tommy, "Now go and get me a pint of best bitter from the 'Three Tuns.'"

Jimmy and Harry fetched the beer and made their old father comfortable. He reached for his pint of beer and took one last long drink.

"Well" he said. "I am off to join the straight faced uns."

He slowly put his beer down on the fireside hob, crossed his arms over his once ample chest and quietly and peacefully departed this life. He was 81 years old.

His boys sat with him for a while then Jimmy said:

"It does not seem right; it'll be the talk of the place that old Tommy Rogers died downstairs and not in his bed." Harry agreed.

"Let's carry him back then."

They carried their father back to bed and laid him out. When the time came for the funeral Tommy had been quite right. It was 'a hell of a job' to get the coffin down the narrow stairs.

Tommy's death was a great loss, not only to his family and friends but to Ironbridge and the surrounding area. He was greatly respected and was a unique character. His like will never be seen again in Ironbridge or anywhere else. People of all classes loved and respected Tommy Rogers of Severnside. His funeral was very well attended by his numerous family and friends.

Talking of their father after his death. Jimmy remarked:

"He went as peaceful as an angel and yet he was one of the toughest hard drinking old beggars that ever walked."

Harry added: "Yes and if he's gone to Heaven I don't know how he did it - but if he's gone to Hell then it's heaven help the Devil!"

Tommy Rogers, countryman, coracle maker, poacher, family man, had departed from his beloved river and his little town of Ironbridge. He was greatly missed.

In 1850 at the time when Tommy and his band were most active in their poaching activies, Ironbridge had over thirty public houses, which gave them a lot of choice as to where to meet up. Such pubs and taverns as were in existence in those days are listed below.

The Bathwell Tavern Head	The Old Queens Vaults, High Street
The Bird in Hand	The Queens Head, Madeley Bank
The Block House	The Railway Tavern
The Bread and Cheese	The Robin Hood
The Chestnuts	The Rodney House
The Coopers Arms	The Royal Oak
The Crown in Waterloo Street	The Station Hotel
The Crown on Hodge Bower	The Swan
The George and Dragon	The Talbot
The Golden Ball	The Three Tuns
The Horse and Jockey	The Tontine
The Lakeshead Tavern	The Unicorn
The Manchester House	The Wheatsheaf
The Meadow	The White Hart
The Old House at Home	The White Horse

James Rogers, born 1886.
(Jimmy, also called 'Dibo')

Jimmy Rogers, Tommy's eldest son, was one of Ironbridge's best loved and highly respected characters. His skill in making and handling the coracle was legendary. He used to show people how to manage the little boat; they could not have found a better tutor. He was also an expert swimmer, and carried on the family tradition of saving people from drowning. For this he received an official Life Saving Award. In World War One, Jimmy was in the navy. His ship was torpedoed in the Gulf of Genoa, and many lives were lost. Swimming for over seven hours, Jimmy and another Ironbridge man, named Luther Bennett, were eventually rescued by a Japanese battleship.

After the war Jimmy worked at the Coalbrookdale Ironworks in addition to his commitment to the river and to coracle making. His countryside skills and love of nature was widely known and the late H S Lloyd, a countryman himself and a breeder of gun dogs said this of Jimmy Rogers:

"A great sportsman, a true friend, and a gentleman to his fingertips. An admirer of beauty and a lover of nature. May his kind never die out."

Jimmy married and had children and grandchildren. They must be very proud of him.

When Jimmy died his ashes were scattered from the Ironbridge on to the waters of the river he knew so well.

Jimmy Rogers and sons at Buildwas.

Luther Bennett, the other Ironbridge man who was in the Navy with Jimmy Rogers, also has an interesting history. His family was connected with the Great Wheel of Benthall, an 18th century corn mill. It was situated across the river, almost opposite the Rogers family home. The wheel looked picturesque amongst the greenery of the woods, especially when it rusted and became covered in moss. It was featured in many paintings and photographs in the 19th and 20th centuries. At one time the mill was used as an abattoir by a local butcher. Luther was the last man to use the energy from the mill to power a generator from which he charged accumulators.

The wheel, fifty feet in diameter, dominated the scenery on the Benthall Bank. It was taken down for scrap metal in 1935. Had it been left it would have become another of the wonders of Ironbridge.

Harry Rogers doing one of his 'stunts' in his coracle. Usually a good crowd of people would gather to watch.

After the death of their father. Jimmy and Harry Rogers carried on the family tradition of coracle making and helping people when the river was in flood. Jimmy was employed full time at the Coalbrookdale Ironworks and Harry worked at a sawmill, and on building sites and farms. The brothers could turn their hands to any type of work. But Jimmy and Harry were countrymen through and through and were proud to follow in their father's footsteps, so relished a night out netting rabbits.

One stormy night Harry planned to go up river. He slung his coracle over his shoulders and with dog and nets set off. He had arranged to meet Nacky Brady on the Ironbridge. He waited awhile but there was no sign of Nacky. It was well past midnight, the wind was getting stronger and it began to rain heavily. He started off alone up the railway line from Ironbridge towards Shrewsbury. The wind was howling down the railway cutting, almost at gale force. Harry stopped, pulled his coracle well over his head and lit up a Woodbine. He enjoyed a few puffs then realised Nacky was beside him.

"Wheer hast thee bin?" demanded Harry.

Nacky mumbled something about the weather and did not seem to be in a very good humour.

"Never mind" said Harry, "Let's get on now."

They struggled on for half an hour, then Harry turned round. There was no Nacky, but the buffers of a goods train were bearing down on him. Alert as usual, he flung himself, dog and coracle down the embankment and the train hurtled by, the driver oblivious that anyone could be on the line. He would not have been able to stop anyway.

Harry began to get worried about Nacky. Suppose he too had not heard the train. He started to walk back down the line. He heard something scrambling about in the withy bushes. It was Nacky, the wind had blown him completely off his feet and down towards the river, where he landed in the withies. The train had rushed by at the same moment.

Nacky was shaken by the experience and also, while down by the withy bushes, he had seen the river at close hand. It was high, very high.

"It's going like a mill race" he told Harry. "If we put our coracles on that we shall surely be drowned." He had had enough of it for one night.

"I'm goin' whum" he said, and turned homewards.

Righto, Nacky" said Harry, always good humoured, and went on with his dog. He had set off intending to catch rabbits and he was not going to be put off. Wind, rain, flooded rivers and hurtling trains were not going to deter Harry. Before the night was out he had a full bag of rabbits. He loaded them into the coracle, and he and his dog went swiftly down the black swirling river. Well before daybreak he was back in his cosy riverside cottage. Several families had rabbit pie for dinner that day. This was the life he loved.

Harry Rogers in his prime near to his workshop on Severnside *c*.1950.

Harry with penny-farthing outside Severn Warehouse *c.*1960.

In Shropshire folklore there is a tale about Old Hippikins the dwarf highwayman, who was said to have been struck dead by lightening. Apparently he haunts the area around Wilderhope, not far from Much Wenlock. Harry was employed by a farmer in that area to catch rabbits on his land. He took his 13 year old son Eusty with him. They were to stay over several days so slept in one of the barns. One night it was so cold and windy that the farmer invited them to sit by the fire and have a cup of tea with himself, his wife and three sons. Harry told them about Hippikins and how his ghost haunted this very farmhouse. When it was time for bed the three boys were quite frightened and instead of each going to his own room, they all slept in one. The farmer suggested that as it was such a wild night. Harry and Eusty could sleep in the house instead of in the barn. Harry was quite happy about this, but young Eusty who had also been frightened by the tale of Hippikins, asked his dad if they could go to sleep in the barn as usual; he was not going to spend the night in a house haunted by the hideous dwarf.

Due to a shortage of jobs in Ironbridge before World War One, Harry went to work in a coal mine near Wrexham. He did not stay very long; he missed the river and Ironbridge too much. While he was there he heard about some coracle racing that was to take place one Saturday on the River Dee. He did not have one of his own boats with him, but he was told he could hire one of the Welsh coracles. These are different from the Ironbridge coracle in that they are pear shaped, while the Ironbridge coracle is round. The broad part of the Welsh coracle is used as the front, with the narrow part of the 'pear' at the back. Harry looked at the coracle and his quick mind got to work. He considered that a Welsh coracle could be propelled through the water 'back to front', i.e. with the narrow part at the front. He went off to find an official who loaned him a coracle and also entered him into the first race at one o'clock. Here Harry's sense of humour took over.

He walked with an awkward gait and struggled to carry the coracle, launching it on the water and pretending to have difficulties in controlling it. The spectators laughed at Harry's attempt to manage the craft. He did everything wrong and even capsized several times. One man asked if he could swim.

"I con swim mate" replied Harry.

At one o'clock, the twenty contestants lined up. The starter's gun went off and Harry with his 'back to front' coracle lost all signs of pretence. He was away, the spectators were amazed at the speed he paddled the coracle. He crossed the winning line well ahead of his nearest rival, a smile on his weather beaten face.

He jumped on shore and walked through the crowds to receive First Prize. They cheered him all the way. One man was angry with him for pretending to be a novice, when he was obviously the most skilful coracle man who had ever entered in a Bangor coracle race.

Harry laughed. "Don't count your chickens before the eggs have hatched next time, mate."

Billy Jones and Harry Rogers at Iron Bridge.

All the Rogers men were expert swimmers: Old Tommy used to swim in the Severn at Ironbridge with Captain Mathew Webb the Channel Swimmer. Harry's friend Billy Jones was also a strong swimmer. Billy's family had a butcher's business in Ironbridge and his father was Mayor of the Ancient Borough of Wenlock. On July 1st 1934, Billy planned to swim down the Severn from Cound to Ironbridge, a distance of 11 miles. He entered the water at 11.30 a.m. He used all his strokes including back stroke, breast stroke and crawl. Harry Rogers accompanied him all the way in his coracle, feeding him with chocolate every now and then. He was never in any difficulty and reached the Rogers landing stage in Ironbridge at eight minutes past 5 p.m.. It had taken him just over five and half hours - a remarkable feat of endurance.

Harry in coracle near to Buildwas.

In 1936 Harry went to a pageant in Ludlow dressed as an ancient Briton. With his rugged, outdoor complexion, his alert eyes and lean tanned body, he must have looked very much like his distant ancestors who sailed the Severn in their coracles centuries ago.

He had many generations of rivercraft bred in him. He was once seen in his coracle gliding casually down from Buildwas with a landing stage and a huge tree trunk in tow. To bring just one of these massive objects down river behind a light craft like the coracle seems almost impossible, but he secured each on ropes and towed them down a river already swollen from recent rain. People watched fascinated as he manoeuvred both with great ease down to his home near the Ironbridge. He pulled in and secured them to some posts. It was a feat worth watching. As one onlooker said,

"Who else but a Rogers could do that?"

When someone had drowned in the Severn, the police always went down the Dip to ask the Rogers family for help in locating the body. This help was available whatever time of day it was or whatever the weather and they accepted no payment for this unpleasant task. It was a family tradition to be of service and they were highly respected because of this.

Anything to do with the river was of interest to Ironbridge people. One day in July 1937 a strange looking craft was spotted coming up the river from Bridgnorth direction. It stopped by the Rogers landing stage and soon attracted interest as it had two parallel floats and an aeroplane propeller at the front. It was in fact a hydro-glider and was the property of Mr. S Bray of Dudley. On board with Mr. Bray were two friends, Mr. F Garbett and Mr. Briscoe of West Bromwich. They were hoping to make it further up river to Shrewsbury, so they asked the well known waterman. Harry Rogers to help pilot the craft. He was interested and prepared to help. It was claimed that the hydro-glider could travel over fords which motor boats could not, and also it was friendly to rowers as it made no wash. It travelled at eight miles an hour. Harry and the crew of the glider set off, but to their disappointment the boat was too wide to get through the weir which was open to rowing boats only. At least they had the experience, and Harry enjoyed handling an unusual craft.

Harry was a born showman and loved to prove his prowess in the coracle. Anyone fortunate enough to have seen him doing some of his stunts on the Severn on a summer's day has seen something that cannot be equalled. He would get the coracle out in mid stream and working the spade (paddle) from the front he would send the boat into a fast spin. It would go round and round, like a water top. By now people had stopped in their tracks to watch the show. With one more skilful flick of the spade he would stop rotating and cause the coracle to lunge to and fro as if jumping waves. Then without warning, he would fall off the plank seat and lie in the bottom of the coracle, put his hands on the back of his head and pretend to go to sleep. Just as suddenly he would leap up and throw the spade twenty yards downstream. It would float swiftly away and Harry would lie as flat as possible in the coracle and paddle with his hand to recover the spade. His favourite stunt was to stand on the plank, and send the coracle into a fast spin. No one else has been known to do this incredible balancing act on a fast river. People loved to watch. He was more at ease on the Severn in his coracle than most people are on dry land.

Harry had known some of the old rivermen of his father's day and as late as 1929 some of the old poachers from those times were still around. One day Sam Beeston, a local waggoner, stopped to feed his horse Boxer, in a field near Ironbridge. There was a haystack in the field from which Sam was going to get the hay for Boxer. He stuck his pikel deep into the stack to lift the hay, when a voice said quietly:

"Watch where theist sticking that pike, mate!"

A head appeared out of the haystack. It was Fussler Potts hiding from the police.

"Hast thee sid any peelers about Sam?" asked Fussler.

"No" Sam replied.

Fussler gave him a pheasant.

"Well if thee dost see any, remember thee hasna sid me."

Nacky Brady was another of the old poachers from Tommy Rogers's time. He was also an excellent basket maker. His baskets were of high quality and the local tradespeople purchased them from him for use on the front of their delivery bicycles. Nacky had been a good swimmer, and an expert coracle man. In his younger days he had saved ten people from drowning. Their names were:

John Boden	George Hill
Sadie Wage	W Woodward
Richard Hill	William Grice
Arthur Bird	John Jones
Mary Wilson	Thomas Morgan

As Nacky grew old and feeble, he could not continue either with his poaching, coracles or his basket making. People were sorry for the old man who had done so much for the community, and an appeal was made. It was worded

FRIENDS AND NEIGHBOURS
We appeal on
Behalf of
An Old Veteran of the River.
He is too old to work now.

The response was excellent. The local people had appreciated what Nacky had done. The community spirit was still there.

Harry on the river in the severe floods of 1946/47 Ironbridge railway station in background.

In 1935 many old cottages in Ironbridge had been condemned by the Borough of Wenlock. Some of these houses were 200 years old. They had no gas, electricity or proper sanitation. They often had an earth lavatory which was shared with another family. Sometimes they had just one large bedroom and a landing bedroom. There was a communal water tap or sometimes a well.

These days, cottages like this would be greatly sought after, with their half timbering, oak beams, inglenook fireplace, flagstone floors, quaint window fastenings and door handles. Those which survived have been bought up and renovated and are now commanding a high price. But in those days the cottages had fallen into disrepair and the people had no money to put things right. The cottages were certainly not suitable for families with several children.

Some modern housing estates had been built, with three and four bedroom properties available, all had modern conveniences including a bathroom which most people had never had or even imagined they could have. Many people were glad to move into these modern houses, but not Harry Rogers. His family had lived at Severnside far too long to be able to settle away from the river. The Severn was their life and had been for over 250 years. He needed to be by the river to make and use his coracles, keep his dogs and ferrets. He told the authorities he would not go and if he was made to, he would 'pick his bearers first'. It was impossible to think of Harry Rogers away from his beloved Severn.

The Rogers' cottage 2007, Eusty Rogers was the last to live there, he died in 2003.

He met with the owner of his cottage and the one next door. It was agreed that Harry could buy both cottages for a nominal sum. The owner and Harry went to a solicitor, papers were signed and it was made legal. Harry was now the owner of the two old cottages. He then saw the local authorities and the sanitary inspector. They told him that if he submitted plans, and the plans were accepted he would be allowed to demolish the two cottages and build one larger house at Severnside.

His brother-in-law, who was a builder and joiner helped to draw up the plans, which were submitted and accepted. Harry was given just three months to build his house. It was to be complete by March 1938 so it was to be done in the winter months of December, January and February.

Harry's family were not afraid of hard work, so they began the task ahead. Harry could put his hand to anything, he had worked at many different trades, including on a building site and at a sawmill. With the help of his family and friends he started on the demolition of the old cottages. They lived in the one whilst they demolished the other.

They worked tirelessly through the day and sometimes by candlelight. They salvaged everything possible from the old houses. Bricks, tiles and quarries were saved. Timber was from Harry's stockyard. Oak that had floated down the river in times of flood had been stored there since Old Tommy's time. The Rogers family and their friends built the house in nine weeks. They named it Victory House with a replica of Nelson's flagship as a door knocker.

Harry on flooded Severn 1946/47 near to Ironbridge Co-op.

In the floods of 1946 and 1947 Harry Rogers did some valuable work for the area. He went out in his coracle to people who were marooned in their homes; many were cut off by the high flood water. The flood water was measured at nineteen feet six inches in the 1946 flood, and just four inches less in 1947. The river came halfway up the Tontine Bank, cutting off shops and houses along the Wharfage. The riverside cottages had flood water in their homes sometimes up to the bedrooms. People standing on the Ironbridge or the Jackfield Bridge could see the carcasses of farm animals being swept down the fast moving river. The water had come up quickly and was relentless in its passage. Fields became lakes and trees at the water's edge had just their top branches showing. Anyone falling in this deep racing water would not have stood a chance. It was frightening to look at, except for one man - Harry Rogers.

flooded fields 1990

Floods 1946/47.

Floods 1946/47.

Floods 1946/47 - these cottages are directly beneath Great Western Railway, embankment top right hand corner.

He launched his coracle, completely fearless of this mass of water and took provisions to people cut off by the flood. Those who were trapped in their bedrooms were rescued by Harry. They must have been frightened climbing into the flimsy little craft, but once they were in they were safe with Harry.

The 'Free' Bridge Jackfield 1946/47 floods.

Several years ago Harry made a broadcast on BBC's Country Magazine. He told of the two miles of Severn where he lived. He explained it was low at present but when it flooded "it was the wickedest stretch of water" he knew. "The banks go up so steep that when it floods the water goes through like a mill race. There's nothing any good on the Severn when it's in flood" he said, "except a coracle, but thee has to know how to handle it." He explained that he was safer in his coracle on the river in the pitch black of night, "than thee bist in this room. I know every yard of it, better than thee knowst this floor."

Ice on the Severn 1980.

He said the only time he was beaten by the Severn was when it was frozen over. It was not possible to take a flimsy coracle amongst all the massive lumps of ice which rumbled down when the thaw set in. "The lumps of ice make the awfullest noise as they crash against each other."

He said that when the thaw came "all manner of tack was going down river with the ice - a good Victorian table, whole trees. It made tears come to me eyes when I saw all that going away."

Harry with Wilfred Byford Jones

The listeners to that programme had the privilege of listening to the old Shropshire dialect spoken by Harry Rogers, coracle man and countryman. He told the BBC of how he had been taught all he knew about the river and the countryside by his father Tommy Rogers. Things like how to knit nets, splice rope, trap game and construct and handle a coracle. He had been a cabin boy on the barges at eight years old and had seen the rough river sailors who thronged the area in those days. He was an expert fisherman. He knew how to tickle trout, catch salmon, lay eel lines. He knew the whereabouts of hawks, herons and when the swan eggs would hatch. He had found out where rare natterjack toads lived, and he knew all about the wildlife which lived by the river and in the fields and woods for miles around. His knowledge of countryside and river lore would fill several books.

He said that going out in the dead of night rabbiting was always an adventure. Sometimes people asked him about his way of life. They seemed fascinated and sometimes asked him to take them out with him on one of his expeditions.

"And the people I mean are well to do people, those who own the land, including the ladies. These landowning ladies wanted to experience the danger and the thrill of going into the remote countryside, into the dark cold loneliness. To kneel at the end of a rabbit net, their hand on the top line waiting for the least tremble, which tells them that the rabbit is entangled in it. These ladies always said they enjoyed the adventure. Yes, they own the land but I have the rabbit catching!"

On a summer evening in the 1950s a bus load of ladies from the West Midlands came on a trip to Ironbridge. The coach pulled up outside The White Hart on the Wharfage as Harry was gliding down river in his coracle. The visitors lined the railings to watch. One woman, braver than the rest, asked Harry for a ride in his coracle.

Harry pulled in and beckoned her to climb aboard. Encouraged by the rest of her friends she got carefully in saying she hoped she would not get wet.

"Thee wusna get wet missus" Harry assured her.

He took her up the Severn for a short distance, which must have been very pleasant on a summer evening, but on the way down he put the coracle into one of his fast spins. The woman screamed so Harry immediately stopped the coracle and paddled her to the side.

"Thank the Lord for that" gasped the lady.

"There you are" said Harry, "dry as a bone."

"No I'm not" laughed the woman, rushing for the nearest toilet.

Harry with Billy Jones daughters in 1946/47 floods.

Harry with his grandchildren, cousins Margaret and Kathleen. These two little girls who are now Mrs. Margaret Seaton-Smith and Mrs. Kathleen Watkiss, gave their approval and help for this book.

Harry Rogers c.1950.

log floating downstream

In 1964 Wilfred Byford Jones visited Severnside and was lucky enough to see Harry at work. As he arrived at Harry's home someone from the other side of the river called "Flotsam!" Everything came to life, dogs barked, rooks started to caw, ferrets ran round their cages.

Harry appeared on the path, and he wore a colourful waistcoat decorated with fishing flies, corduroy trousers, leggings and a rabbit's foot in his cap. He launched the coracle and Byford Jones was treated to a rare sight. Harry paddled to midstream as a massive tree came swirling down the river. He drew alongside it, and knocked a nail in it to which was attached a rope. Paddling the coracle with one hand, he calmly pulled the monster tree into the bank and secured it. Someone watching said "You will not see that done anywhere else."

Byford Jones was invited to see Harry's 'graveyard' where he stored the wood he had rescued from the river. There were massive tree trunks, ancient oak beams and farm gates, and an old fruit barrow. As they talked a pet fox sauntered in and rubbed his nose on Harry's leg just like a dog.

"Hello Billy" said Harry stroking the fox. The fox looked up affectionately at the old coracle man. "He goes off sometimes" explained Harry, "but he always come back at night for his dinner."

Harry had a friend by the name of Jack Gears. It was an apt name for this man as he was extremely clever with anything of a mechanical nature. In 1959 it was the 250th Anniversary of the Coalbrookdale Ironworks. Harry and Jack knew that a lot of people would be coming to the area for this celebration, so they decided to do something 'special'.

They erected a high wire across and high above the Severn. Jack made a device which was worked by the current of the river. He also made two figures, one of a man on a one-wheeled bicycle and the other of a witch on a broomstick. Harry and Jack attached the witch and the cyclist to the high wire, which was then connected to Jack's device in the water. As soon as the visitors began to pour in, they set the device working and the witch flew across the river on her broomstick, and a few minutes later a little man went across on his one-wheeled cycle. The visitors standing on the bridge were just as fascinated by these two models as they were by the Ironbridge itself.

The Dip - Severnside.

The landing stage situated on the river at Severnside had been made by and was the property of the Rogers family. It was ideal to stand on for fishing and providing people asked permission to use it, they were never refused. One day Harry and his son Eusty had been doing a backbreaking dirty job of clearing out the cellars under one of the old shops in Ironbridge. This cellar had obviously not been cleared out for many years, but Harry and Eusty were never afraid of hard work. They laboured for hours in the dark grimy conditions. During carrying out the rubbish. Harry noticed a man, a complete stranger; go down the Dip towards the river. After half an hour or so, Harry followed him. Sure enough the man was standing on Harry's landing stage, fishing. Harry, covered from head to foot in dirt from the cellar asked the man,

"Had any luck mate?"

"No" said the fisherman, "I haven't had a bite and I am fed up."

"I am fed up too" said Harry, "1 am fed up with working my guts out, coming home to a nagging wife, fed up with the low wages, with the politicians, and the whole bloody lot. I have had enough of this wicked world and I'm getting out of it."

With that he leapt fully clothed, with his cap still on, into the deep waters of the Severn and disappeared, leaving the horrified fisherman on the landing stage. Swimming under water for fifty yards or so. Harry surfaced further down and hid under some withy bushes. He watched in glee as the angler stared in amazement at the river, before packing up his fishing rods and running back to the Dip.

Several months later Harry was sitting on the railings just above the landing stage, when the same fisherman appeared on the path. He caught sight of Harry and stopped in his tracks, white-faced and mouth open. Harry gave a little smile "No I'm not a ghost, but I might have been for all the help you were prepared to give last time you were down here." Harry had a sense of humour, but he felt that the visitor needed to be taught a lesson.

Harry had been a part of Ironbridge life for so long it was impossible to imagine the small market town without him. For so many years people had been used to seeing him paddling his coracle on the Severn, or sitting on the wall by the market square with his pet fox on his lap. The fox would take sweets out his mouth to the amusement of visitors.

It was said that when David O Selsnick made the film 'Gone to Earth' in Shropshire, it was Harry Roger's fox which played the part of Toxy' which Jennifer Jones, (Hazel Wood) carried about with her. This is quite likely as Harry's fox was so tame it would be quite at ease with film stars and camera men. Other people think the fox was from an animal sanctuary.

Eusty Rogers, *c*.1960.

Harry with pet fox *c*.1950.

Jimmy and Harry the fearless brothers, c.1950.

As he sat on the market square wall Harry looked every inch a countryman with his fancy waistcoat, fishing flies attached, his cap with a rabbit's foot his corduroys and sometimes puttees on his legs. In old age his eyes were bright and alert, his conversation lively with ready wit, and all in the old Shropshire dialect. He had enjoyed life and had always lived at his home in Severnside which he had built himself with the help of family and friends.

He died in 1967 at the age of 80. The people of Ironbridge missed him greatly. He and his family had been of great service to the community. His son Eusty would carry on the tradition.

The Dip, 2006.

Eustace Rogers (Eusty) 1914-2002

Eusty's father Harry Rogers died in 1967, and eighteen months later his mother passed away, and Eusty was left alone in the family home on Severnside. It was a sad time for him but he was kept busy as he was then working full time at Ironbridge Power Station and also making the traditional type coracles of ash slats and pitched and tarred calico.

One day as he was working in his garden constructing a coracle, a visitor arrived at his gate. The man introduced himself to Eusty and asked whether he had ever made a coracle from animal skins like the ones the Ancient Britons had used. He told Eusty about one he had seen in a Scottish museum. The coracle man was interested and told the visitor he would "have a go". He obtained some bullock hide from a local abattoir and dried and cured it over several days. No one had told him about how to go about the procedure, but coracle making, from whatever material, was in his blood. He stretched the hide over a framework of willow wands and secured everything together with horsehair rope. The silky fur of the bullock was the 'inside' of the coracle, and Eusty left the tail hanging on it. The outside, which was to be in contact with the water, was completely waterproof and did not need to be tarred and pitched as it would with calico. Eusty always said,

"Everything comes from nature. This is how primitive man made his boat. He made it this way, because it is the best way. The shape of the hide makes the shape of the boat."

He constructed several of these primitive types of coracles. One went to New Zealand but the transport costs were so high, no more were shipped there. One went to a museum in Scotland, and he kept one in his workshop to show to visitors.

He continued to make the traditional coracles, but in winter when it was too cold to work in his garden, he sat by his kitchen fire and made a third type, a miniature coracle. It was tarred and pitched just like the larger ones, and these small coracles were very popular. He gave some away to family and friends, and a great many to charity. He could have made a lot of money by selling these small boats but, as he said, it was a hobby. He was doing something he liked and at the same time helping others.

Eusty Rogers, *c.*1950.

Eusty Rogers, *c.*1950.

Eusty once sold one of his large traditional coracles to a high ranking army officer. He offered to give the purchaser some lessons in the coracle before he took it away. The soldier assured Eusty that he would be able to manage this small craft. A week later the officer appeared down the Dip to see Eusty, explaining that he had not found it so easy after all, and would Eusty please give him a few hints. Eusty was only too happy to oblige and gave the officer all the tuition he required.

When he sold one of his coracles to a novice, he was just as conscientious as his father, Harry, who used to say "Con yer swim?" Eusty explained to the buyer that handling a coracle is not easy. "You have to know what you are doing". As there is no keel to steady it, it is difficult to get into. Beginners tend to take it to shallow water, and then their weight forces it to the bottom where the covering is damaged. Regarding paddling it, the ordinary way of paddling does not work, the coracle would simply go round and round. He would tell the novice to place the paddle (or spade as he called it) as far away as possible from the side of the coracle and to draw it in to the side. He would also tell them "The coracle is not a plaything. Try it on a canal at first. You cannot come to much harm on a canal!" Once the art of managing a coracle is mastered it can be used in many situations, as in the old days when the river men went to lay eel lines it was invaluable.

When Eusty retired from Ironbridge Power Station he still had plenty to occupy him. He gave talks to school children, telling them of life by the river, and of the floods which had devastated the area over the years. The worst on record was in 1795 when the river was 29 feet above its normal level. In more recent times the worst was in the winter of 1946 and early 1947. There had been heavy snow for weeks and when it melted the river rose by nine feet. During this flood the Rogers coracle men took food and coal to those cut off by the rising water. However high the river, the coracle men would still set out. They were fearless and dedicated to helping the marooned families.

The tourists liked to go down the Dip and listen to Eusty's stories of the Severn Gorge, tales handed down by his father and grandfather. Old Tommy Rogers, Eusty's grandfather could remember the trowmen and bargemen taking goods down to Gloucester and Bristol. His grandfather had related tales of the old Ironbridge taverns, smoky, low beamed places, with spittoons and sawdust on the floor. The beer was good and there was a fire to sit by but some tough characters drank there, and fights sometimes broke out.

Eusty also told the visitors of how the coracle men took people over the river to save them paying the halfpenny toll. A halfpenny does not sound much but in those hard times, it was a lot for poor family. He also related the adventures of the old poachers. These men spent nights out in the cold dark woods, netting rabbits, then came down the river in the dead of night in their coracles.

"Why did they do it?" one visitor asked.

"To live! To live!" Eusty would exclaim. "They did it to live. The poachers put a meal on the table for hungry families" Eusty told of how all of the Rogers family would help to construct coracles. "We all took a hand in it" he said, "There was no getting out of it."

Eusty had been interviewed on radio and television. Journalists from local and national newspapers had gone down the Dip to see the coracle man.

In 1981 Catherine Watson, the Travel Adventure editor of the American newspaper 'The Minneapolis Tribune' came to see Eusty as she needed material to write an article about coracles. People of all nationalities came to see Eusty and enjoy the peace of the riverside. They must have been fascinated by his wealth of information about the river and the old town of Ironbridge. Some would remember his father Harry and his prowess in the coracle. Eusty recalled how Harry had once sold a coracle to an American Naval Officer who was serving on the Polaris in Holy Loch. This officer, who served on one of the most modern craft invented, was the proud owner of a replica of the most ancient boat known on British rivers.

In 1970 HRH Princess Margaret came to the district and toured the Ironbridge Gorge Museums. She officially opened the Coalport Canal, which had been restored by the museum. In 1928 the canal had been filled in due to a cholera outbreak. The restoration had started in 1969, rubble from the canal dug out, and the whole are landscaped. The canal runs through the old Coalport China works. After excavation it was repuddled and filled with water. It was then how it had been in the days when barges and trows went up and down the Severn. After the Princess had officially opened the canal, Eusty Rogers presented her with one of his miniature coracles. His father and grandfather would have been proud of him.

In 1979 the committee of the local Methodist church asked Eusty if he would convey two of their ministers over the Severn to commemorate the 200th Anniversary of the crossing of the river by their founder member, John Wesley in 1779. Eusty was pleased to do this and even constructed a new landing stage for this special occasion. So on March 20th 1979, the Rev Davies and the Rev Kinch were ferried across the river, from the site of the old White Brickworks. Eusty and his friend Philip Barnes manned the punt and steered it under theIronbridge on its way to the landing stage.

As in 1779, a sermon was preached on the Broseley side, and after landing in Ironbridge the ministers proceeded to the chapel at Madeley Wood. This was the 'new' chapel, built in 1837. The old chapel which John Wesley visited in 1779 had stood nearby. The local Methodists were delighted with this re-enactment, thanks in a great part to Eusty Rogers.

In 1979 Prince Charles also came to Ironbridge to unveil a plaque to commemorate the bicentenary of the bridge. The town was decorated with flags and bunting and people turned out in their hundreds to welcome the Prince. He walked over the bridge and after paying his toll, unveiled the plaque. He then had a 'walkabout' greeting various people including Ironbridge's oldest resident, Mrs. Beddoes. Prince Charles then went down Severnside to see Eusty on the river in his coracle. Did the Prince wish he could 'have a go' at handling a coracle? Perhaps.

In March 1980 seven young nurses, finalists in the 'Nurse of the Year Award' arrived in Ironbridge with Leslie Crowther as compere, and Jean Morton as producer. It was hoped that Eusty would be able to take one of the nurses on the river in his coracle. Unfortunately that day the river was high and racing through the Gorge and it was considered too dangerous to take the young nurse out in such conditions, but to avoid disappointment they all went up to Holmer Lake, a distance of around two miles away. There Eusty took her on the lake in his coracle. She was rather nervous.

"Don't worry" said Eusty, "I've done this before."

Eusty was usually to be found in his garden on summer days talking to visitors from all over the world. He was never tired of telling them about coracles, and of the rivermen, and the tourists were never tired of listening. In the evening when the visitors had gone, he would lean on the railings overlooking the river and chat to his old friends. His garden was full of relics of the past, old dog kennels, ferret cages, wheel barrows and huge tree trunks which his father or grandfather had dragged out of the river as they paddled their coracles.

It was relaxing and peaceful by the riverside on those summer evenings. Eusty was getting old so he enjoyed the quiet time watching the river on which he, and his father and grandfather had handled the little coracle so skilfully. He could see the beautiful greenery of Ladywood opposite, brilliant in the setting sun, woods which he and his family knew as well as their own back yard. It was on such an evening that I went to see Eusty, the time when I was shown the treasures of his workshop. During the course of our conversation, I asked him about the well-known personalities who had come to see him.

"What was it like talking to Princess Margaret that day back in 1970?" I asked.

"Just like talking to you," he said, "just like talking to you."

Eusty and friends on a quiet summer evening on Severnside, 1984.

WÄRNING!
This River is extremely
DANGEROUS
nd _not_ suitable for Bathing

Eusty on Severnside, 1995, (photo Diane Perry).

Eusty died on January 31st 2003 aged 88. He was the last coracle man of Ironbridge. St. Luke's Church, high above the town, was filled to capacity. His coffin, on which was placed one of his miniature coracles, was followed by his sisters, and other family members. Not just family and local friends attended, but people from other parts of Shropshire's countryside came to pay their respects. Eusty was held in high esteem as was his grandfather, Tommy, and father. Harry, and Uncle Jimmy.

From the churchyard the mourners could see the thickly wooded slopes of Benthall and Ladywood. These woods, the old Bridge and the Severn were an important part of Eusty's life. Now he was gone from them.

Visitors to Ironbridge will never again see Eusty in his garden on a summer's day, making a coracle a smile on his humorous face and ready to talk about life by the Severn. No more will the fearless brothers. Jimmy and Harry, launch their coracles on the river, and set off on the treacherous water to rescue people from drowning or to take provisions to those cut off by the flood. And in the dead of night there is no Tommy Rogers gliding silently down the dark river, his coracle full of rabbits he had netted in the lonely woods.

The Rogers family home has been sold, the garden cleared of those relics which floated down the Severn so long ago. The local dialect with its 'thee bist' and 'yo canna' and 'get thee whum' delivered in the Shropshire drawl with a slight Welsh lilt, is rarely heard now. Once the little market town was filled with this distinctive speech, as it was filled with characters whose like will never be seen again, for Nacky Brady, Gunner Boden, Bunkus Owen, Hell Fire Jack, Tommy, Harry, Jimmy, and Eusty Rogers and the rest of the coracle men are gone.

Just as the river flows through Ironbridge and then passes on, these men too have passed on... But they made their mark - these 'Gentlemen of the River'. Their bond with the Severn was so strong; their spirit will remain in the valley forever.

(photo Paul Bond)

The New Coracle Men and Women

The coracle was a working boat for the old rivermen of Ironbridge for many centuries. These men have now passed away, but the art of coracle making and handling has been revived in the Severn Gorge. In Wales too, the coracle is still used on the rivers Dee, Teifi, Towy and many others. When Shrewsbury Town Football Club played on the old Gay Meadow, any footballs landing in the river were retrieved by Fred Davies in his coracle, before the ball floated down to the Bristol Channel!

Thanks to the Green Wood Centre of Coalbrookdale coracles are again afloat on the river at Ironbridge, keeping up the tradition of the old coraclemen of the Severn Gorge.

The present day coracles are constructed at the Green Wood Centre under the tuition of Terry Kenny. Groups of people, several times a year, are taught the art of coracle making. About forty coracles are completed every year. Then the exciting time arrives when the student takes his or her hand-made coracle down to the river, to launch it on the beautiful but challenging Severn.

On August Bank Holiday enthusiasts from different parts of the country arrive at the Regatta Field in Ironbridge for the Annual Coracle Race, organized by the Green Wood Centre and the Ironbridge Lions Club.

There are a great many entrants, and it's a wonderful day out. The new coracle people are proficient and keen - the old rivermen of Ironbridge would be impressed.

So the art of making and handling coracle is not lost. Good luck to the little boats and all who sail in them.

The Greenwood Centre Coalbrookdale, (Photo Phyllis Blakemore 2009).